Bible Encyclopedia
A first reference book

By Etta Wilson and Sally Lloyd Jones
Illustrated by Steven D. Schindler

STANDARD
PUBLISHING
Cincinnati, Ohio

Animals

To people who lived in Bible times, animals were very helpful. People used animals for food, clothing, transportation and labor, but not many animals were kept as pets. Animals in Bible stories also can teach us important things. For example, Jesus compared people who are lost from God to sheep who are lost from their shepherd.

God's people did not worship animals like the Egyptians and Greeks did. They knew God created all the animals. But God gave his people rules about taking care of animals. For example, if a person found a donkey or an ox that had fallen down, God wanted him to help the animal to its feet. (See Deut. 22:4.)

He was a mighty ratter.

Egyptians buried their cats in special cat cemeteries.

People admired eagles because they lived in high places and had very keen eyesight. (See Isaiah 40:31.)

Wild wolves lived in the hills.

Camels can go without drinking water for up to two weeks. So they could make long trips across the desert.

Airmail in Bible times

Doves Ltd.

Can I get a message to Bethel overnight?

You're in luck. I've got one dove left.

Bethel

Nazareth

Doves are symbols of peace. They were also mail carriers in Bible times! They could fly a long way and always found the way home.

Goats were useful animals. Their skin was used for making water bottles, and their hair could be made into clothing or tents. And don't forget milk and cheese!

Foxes usually lived in holes or burrows made by other animals. They were pests – they ate the grapes in vineyards.

The Pharaoh of Egypt forced the Hebrew people to be slaves. So God filled all of Egypt with frogs as a punishment.

Cats were especially loved in Egypt where they were given very special treatment.

Sometimes poor people sacrificed sparrows instead of a lamb.

Ants are such hard workers that they were a good example for their human neighbors! (See Proverbs 6:6.)

"Eat your heart out, Maybelline!"

Camels' bushy eyebrows kept the sand out of their eyes!

"Sure, I bite when I'm stepped on. Is that so wrong?"

In Bible times, snakes were a symbol of evil.

"This is great, especially after the week I've had!"

Animals had a day of rest each week, just like people did!

Locusts for lunch?

"Eat my figs, will ya? Catch another 50 of you guys and I'll have enough for a locust pie!"

Locusts liked to eat every plant in sight. They could destroy a crop in hours. But people ate the locusts, too — boiled, fried or dried!

Sheep everywhere!

"I know mares eat oats and does eat oats, but lambs eat grass!"

Sheep were plentiful in Bible lands. Before Jesus came, God's people brought perfect lambs to sacrifice to pay for their sins. Jesus is called the "Lamb of God" because he died to take away everyone's sins.

The cock's crow

"Oh, man! Where is that bum?!"

Soldiers used roosters to signal when to change guard.

Wild bears were dangerous. King David killed a bear to protect his sheep.

Donkeys carried heavy loads and were used for pulling plows. In peace time kings rode on donkeys instead of horses.

Lions roamed wild in the forests of Canaan. Three of the tribes of Israel used a lion as their symbol because lions were so strong and brave.

Oxen needed a lot of pasture and grain so only rich people kept them.

Sea monster!

"Wouldn't you know? I left my big net at home."

The Bible mentions a huge sea creature called a "leviathan" (Isaiah 27:1). No one knows for sure what it looked like, but you can bet it was pretty scary!

Buildings

In Bible lands, most houses and shops were very small and simple. Wood was scarce, so buildings were made from stone and mud. But some cities had temples and synagogues that were large and beautiful. And in Rome, people lived in tall, poorly built apartment buildings that sometimes collapsed!

Many communities were surrounded by strong walls with gates that were locked at night. These walls protected the people from the attacks of armies and outlaws.

Unless they were wealthy, families lived in one-room houses. In the winter, families brought their sheep, goats and chickens inside, too!

This scene shows us what buildings looked like in Jesus' time.

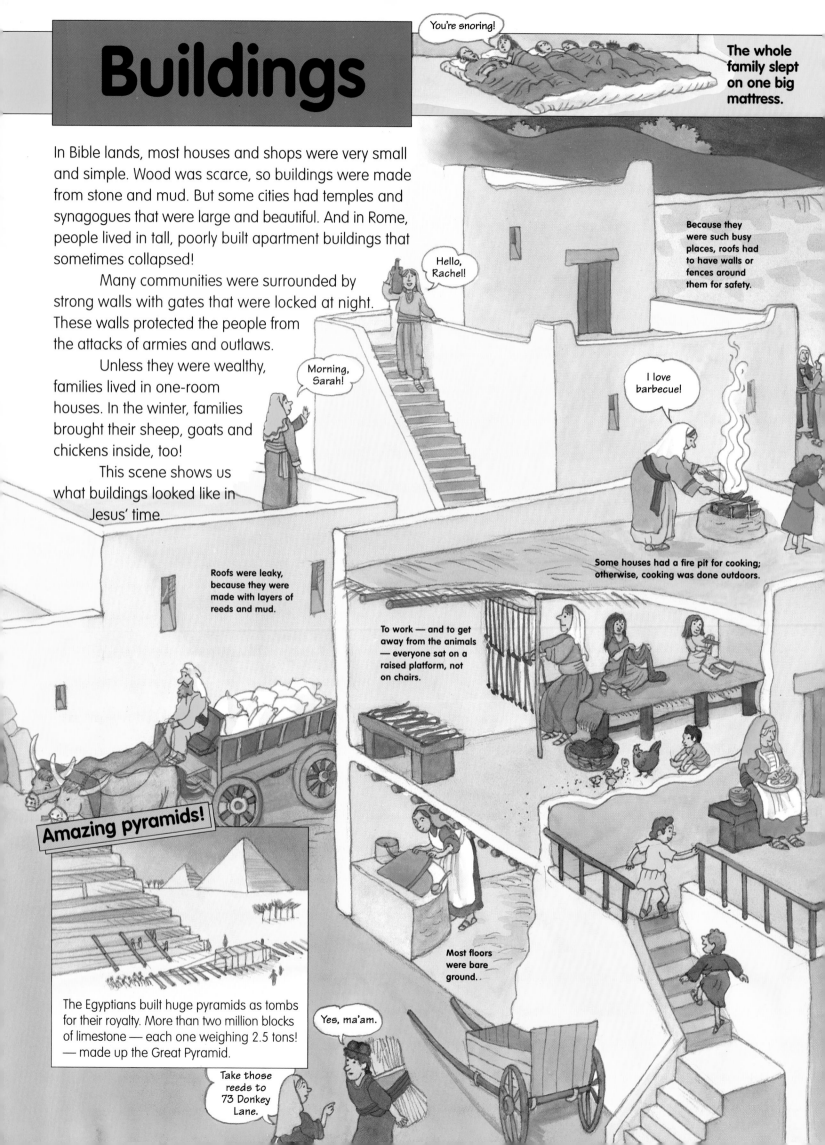

You're snoring!

The whole family slept on one big mattress.

Hello, Rachel!

Because they were such busy places, roofs had to have walls or fences around them for safety.

Morning, Sarah!

I love barbecue!

Some houses had a fire pit for cooking; otherwise, cooking was done outdoors.

Roofs were leaky, because they were made with layers of reeds and mud.

To work — and to get away from the animals — everyone sat on a raised platform, not on chairs.

Amazing pyramids!

Most floors were bare ground.

The Egyptians built huge pyramids as tombs for their royalty. More than two million blocks of limestone — each one weighing 2.5 tons! — made up the Great Pyramid.

Yes, ma'am.

Take those reeds to 73 Donkey Lane.

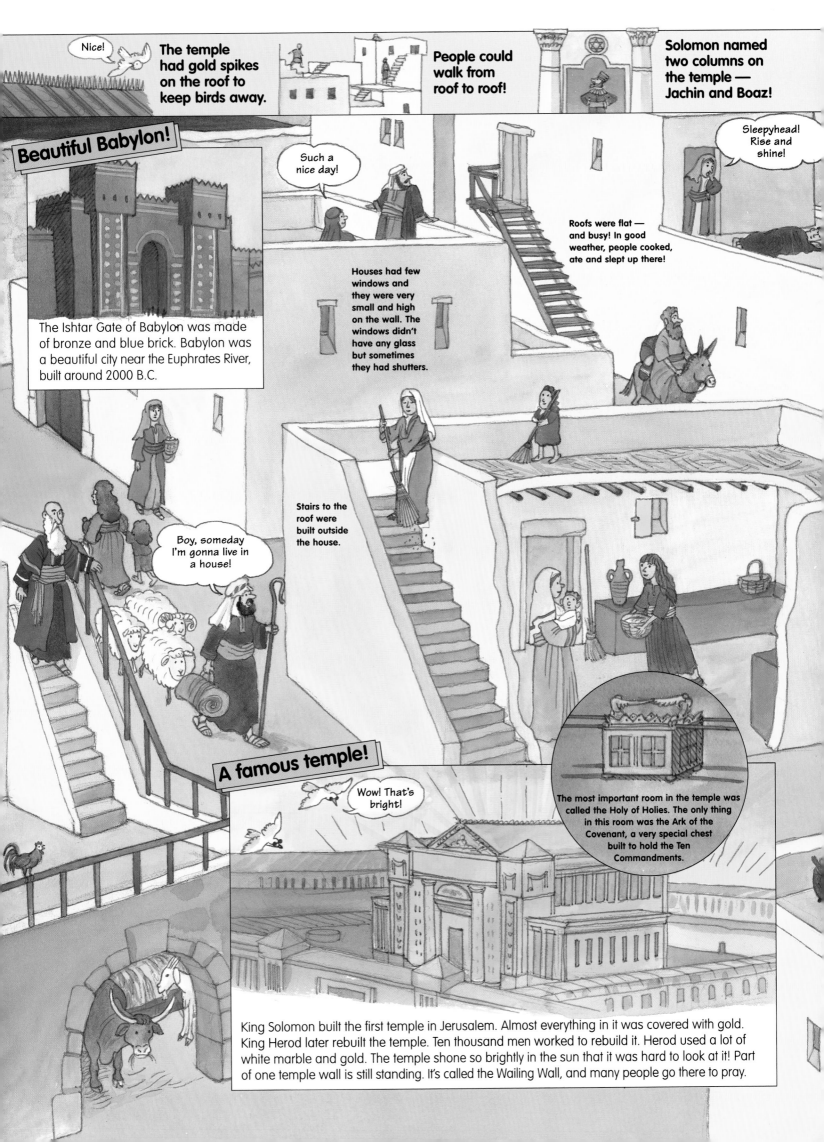

Nice!

The temple had gold spikes on the roof to keep birds away.

People could walk from roof to roof!

Solomon named two columns on the temple — Jachin and Boaz!

Sleepyhead! Rise and shine!

Beautiful Babylon!

Such a nice day!

Roofs were flat — and busy! In good weather, people cooked, ate and slept up there!

Houses had few windows and they were very small and high on the wall. The windows didn't have any glass but sometimes they had shutters.

The Ishtar Gate of Babylon was made of bronze and blue brick. Babylon was a beautiful city near the Euphrates River, built around 2000 B.C.

Boy, someday I'm gonna live in a house!

Stairs to the roof were built outside the house.

A famous temple!

Wow! That's bright!

The most important room in the temple was called the Holy of Holies. The only thing in this room was the Ark of the Covenant, a very special chest built to hold the Ten Commandments.

King Solomon built the first temple in Jerusalem. Almost everything in it was covered with gold. King Herod later rebuilt the temple. Ten thousand men worked to rebuild it. Herod used a lot of white marble and gold. The temple shone so brightly in the sun that it was hard to look at it! Part of one temple wall is still standing. It's called the Wailing Wall, and many people go there to pray.

Clothes

People in Bible times wore loose clothing. They had to — the climate in Palestine was very warm! When the weather turned cool at night and in the winter, people put on several layers of clothes. In summer and winter, everybody wore a tunic, which was like a long T-shirt. Tunics were belted at the waist. Clothing was made of leather, wool, goat hair, camel hair or cotton. Priests and rich people wore clothes made of linen.

Do you like purple, red, yellow and blue? So did people in Bible times! They made purple dye from snails, red dye from oak trees and insects, yellow dye from almonds and blue dye from pomegranates. The purple dye was hard to make and very expensive. So only rich people — usually kings and queens — wore purple. Everyone liked red — except the Egyptians, who thought red was unlucky.

This scene set in Palestine shows what people wore during Jesus' time.

Gee! Who would have guessed? It looks hot!

Egyptian pharaohs sometimes wore fake beards made of gold!

When a Jewish person was sad, because someone had died or because he had done something wrong, he wore a rough cloth called sackcloth.

Some Jews wore Greek or Roman clothes, such as togas, to be fashionable.

Did you hear? Eli has carpal tunnel bad!

Oh, no!

Roman soldiers wore sandals with iron hob nails on the soles that made marching easier. They carried short swords for battle.

There's a guy on Shalom Street who fixes hob-nailed sandals. Mine march like brand-new!

Scribes wore inkhorns in their belts.

Buy it new!

Oh, yes! All our tunics are brand new! See? No head hole!

Eli's Custom Tunics

Talliths were tunics that some Jews wore as a sign that they were different from other people. Talliths were sold with no hole for the head. That way, the buyers knew if they were getting new ones!

Sandals were made from wood or dried grasses woven together and tied on with a leather strip.

Food

"Your favorite — honey and carob!"

Beans were used for baking. Imagine a bean birthday cake!

People in Bible lands usually ate well, unless a drought or insects ruined the crops. Farmers grew grains, vegetables, fruits, nuts, spices and herbs. And there was plenty of fish, milk, butter and cheese to eat. Most people ate meat only on special occasions.

God's people followed special laws about eating meat and fish. They could eat meat only from animals that had split hooves and ate grass, like cows and goats. They could eat only fish that had scales and fins. They were not allowed to eat pork or shellfish. This protected them from getting sick, because these foods often cause food poisoning if they are not kept or prepared carefully.

Digging for salt

"Do you want to help, Simon?"

"Sure! Looks like fun!"

People collected salt by digging a hole in the sand near the sea and letting the water evaporate. Then they collected the salt that was left behind.

Honey

ink

Among the Jewish people, crushed garlic was a favorite spread on bread. Everybody ate it, so no one noticed the smell!

Plants provided more than food. People used the rush (or reed) plant to make walking sticks, fishing poles, flutes, baskets, mats and even paper and pens!

"Yikes!"

"Oh, yummy. Honey!"

Slaves extracted honey from beehives by smoking the bees out first.

"Oh, dear! These are a little too brown!"

"More milk?"

People kept milk in a bottle made of goat skin. But they couldn't keep milk for long because they didn't have refrigerators.

Instead of a table, food was placed on the floor on a leather or skin cloth. And people sat on the floor, not on chairs.

"Yes, please!"

Bread was the most important food at every meal, and women baked bread almost every day. Most people used barley, which was cheaper. Only wealthy people used wheat. (See Luke 9 for a story about five barley loaves!)

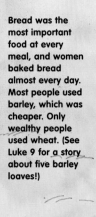

"Thank you, Lord. It was very tasty!"

The Jewish people gave thanks before and after a meal.

"Does it look really gross?"

A favorite dish was sheep's tails!

"Hmmm – a bit more honey!"

Toothpaste was made of ground oyster shells and honey!

From milk to cheese

"See? It hardens and then just pops out!"

"Neat!"

SALT

Cheese was made by stirring salt into goat's milk and then letting the mixture sit in the sun to harden.

Something's fishy!

"Well, at least we'll have a nice sunny day for this!"

"Phew!"

Fish was almost as important as bread. Since they had no refrigerators, people kept fish from rotting by salting and drying it in the sun.

The Israelites liked figs and ate them fresh, dried, or pressed into cakes.

"Try this cake, sweetie. It's made out of figs and honey."

Sugar didn't grow in Bible lands. So people used honey to sweeten their food.

People liked pomegranates, including the juice.

Watermelons were a good source of water in dry spells.

Big clusters of grapes grew up to 12 pounds! People ate grapes fresh, or dried as raisins, and they squeezed the juice to make vinegar and wine.

"Umph!"

"Whack it hard!"

People harvested olives by beating the tree with a long stick.

"Bekka, please pass the salt."

Salt was used for many things, and the Dead Sea was full of it! People seasoned food with salt, and sealed promises by sharing salt. They even rubbed it on newborn babies to kill germs.

The useful olive

"Yum!"

PRESS

"Ahh!"

A single olive tree could grow enough olives to make a family's oil for a whole year! This oil was used for cooking, burning in lamps and for soothing cuts and bruises, as well as for preparing a body for burial.

Jobs

It would take a tailor thirteen years to weave a robe out of gold!

I hope this doesn't go out of fashion before I finish it!

In Bible times people worked very hard for little pay. Most people worked outdoors and got a lot of exercise! Farming, fishing and sheep tending were popular trades. Some tradesmen, such as carpenters and tentmakers, had shops in towns and cities where they could sell their products.

Usually only the men had trades, but women worked hard taking care of their families, homes and land. And grown-ups weren't the only ones who labored. Boys and girls worked hard, too.

This busy village scene shows people working at some of the typical jobs in Bible times.

Fishermen worked hard! They rowed their heavy boats and worked through the night catching fish. In the daytime, they prepared the fish to sell and repaired their nets.

Lousy! Just minnows!

How'd ya do last night?

Here we are, little fella!

Baaa!

Baaa!

Shepherds lived with their flocks of sheep and protected them. They used their crooks to keep the sheep from danger.

Don't be smelly!

Oh, my! That really gets in your nose!

People didn't take many baths in Bible times; there wasn't much water to go around. So they needed perfumers to make them smell a little better! Perfumers dipped flowers into very hot, melted fat to make a nice-smelling ointment.

Bricks made of mud and straw were molded into rectangles, then left in the sun to bake.

Wood was scarce in Bible lands. So carpenters had to work well with stone, as well as with wood.

Dad, do you like stone work?

See? You *can* saw stone!

Scribes wrote letters for people who couldn't write.

Dear Sirs: . . .

Pots were in great demand, so potters were busy spinning, shaping and painting clay.

Jewelers purified clay by melting it, then blowing on it through a pipe to clean the impurities.

The smith made axes, metalware and ploughs for people.

A fuller cleaned clothes by stepping on them!

Simon, take a letter.

Most secretaries were men.

These are termite proof!

Sometimes carpenters made teeth out of wood!

Tanners made leather from animal skins. This process was so smelly that tanners lived outside towns and cities.

Fetching water was difficult, since most towns were built on hills. Springs were usually at the base of a hill, so women had to carry full jars uphill.

Children enjoyed stomping through piles of grapes in the press to make wine.

Eek!

Lunch time!

Lunch time!

Traveling merchants sold their goods — silk, ivory, spices, monkeys — at the city gate.

Gatekeepers were called "porters." They guarded the entrances to cities, public buildings and rich people's houses.

Zzzz...

Elias, I've been hearing rumors about you...

Who, me?

CASH Express

Visitors from other countries exchanged their currency for local money through money changers. Money changers often cheated.

The inspector oversaw people's trades to make sure that they were being honest.

Water into stone?

Here's the water, Dad!

Splash them good, son!

Works every time!

Wow!

SNAP!

Here's how stoneworkers got the stone they used for buildings, statues and water wells. First, they cut big chunks of stone from a quarry. Then they pounded wooden wedges into the stone and soaked the wedges with water. When they swelled, the wedges cracked the stone into pieces.

Healing arts

Doc, this bill seems a little high.

Within the law! Hey, I've got overhead. I'm just about breaking even!

Mesopotamians were strict with their doctors. Their laws limited how much a doctor could charge for his work. And any doctor who was caught being careless had to pay a penalty. In the field of surgery, the Egyptians were the best. They later passed on their great knowledge to the Greeks.

School

Just like it is today, school was important in Bible times. The first schools may have been in Sumeria (which is Iraq today), 2,500 years before Jesus was born. The Sumerians invented the first writing system.

Jewish children started going to school when they were about five years old, and left school when they were about fifteen. But school was not a requirement. If fathers needed their sons to help at home, the boys didn't have to go to school.

School was in session all year. And the school day was very long, starting at sunrise. Often there was a break in the hot afternoon.

Students mostly studied the Scriptures, law and history, and they learned to read from scrolls. But during Jesus' lifetime, there were Roman schools, with slaves as teachers, which taught many other subjects: philosophy, music, language, poetry, math, engineering, law — and even dancing!

This scene shows a typical class of Jewish boys during the time of Jesus.

How's this, Dad?

Yikes!

Shepherd boys learned to use slingshots to protect their sheep.

Part of the Jewish lesson was called "question and answer period."

The teachers in Jewish schools were called "rabbis." Rabbis also taught their students how to get along with others.

Simeon, are you trying to tell me that the goat ate your homework again?

Teachers wrote on wax-coated wooden boards that could be rubbed clean.

To help a boy learn, his teacher gave him a personal text that started with the first letter of the boy's name and ended with the last!

Teachers were not allowed to eat, drink or joke with the students!

Oohh, oohh! Rabbi!

Boys of different ages were in the same class.

Boy, h smar

Like father, like son

I think a few more whacks of the chisel and this'll fit!

Do you think Mom will like her new door?

In addition to their studies at school, boys learned their fathers' trades. For example, Jesus learned to be a carpenter because Joseph was a carpenter. A boy who didn't know a trade was thought to be a thief! As well as teaching him a trade, a father had to find his son a wife and teach him to swim!

That Levi is such a showoff!

Papyrus, which was made of dried papyrus plant, was expensive, so students usually wrote on clay tablets.

Although wealthy children went to school with everyone else, sometimes they also had tutors at home.

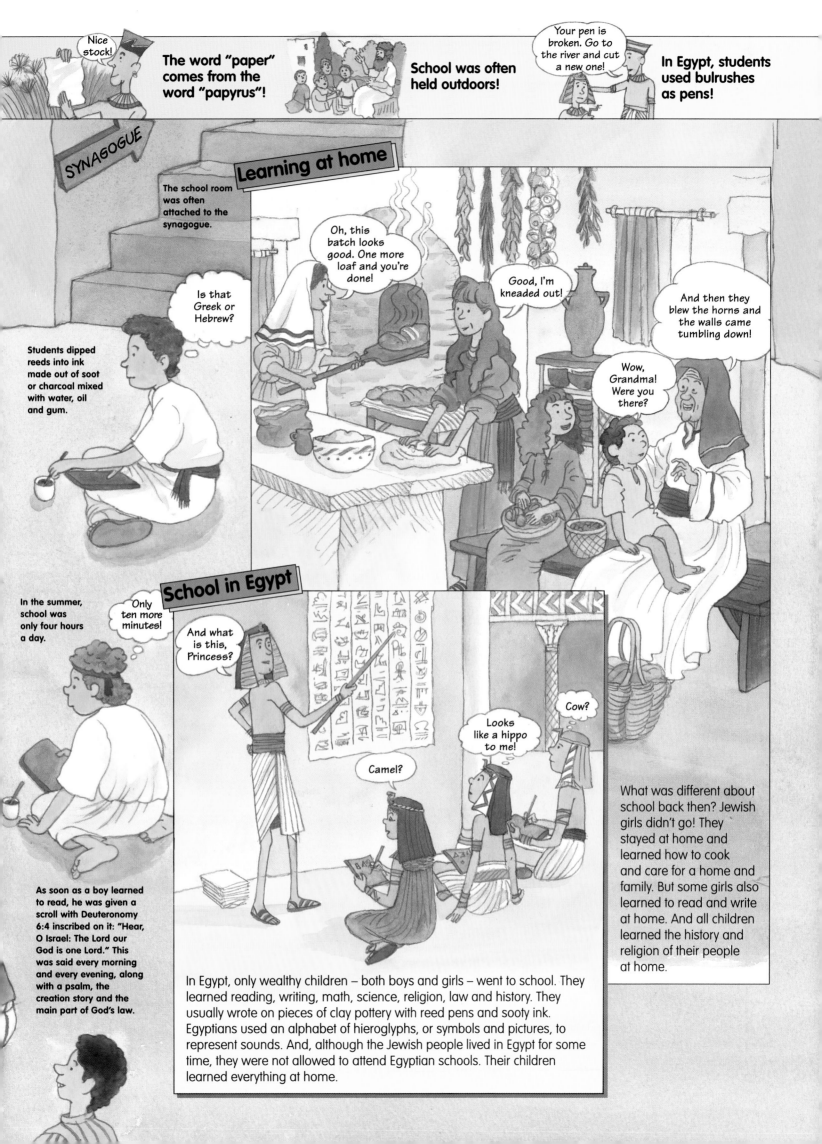

The word "paper" comes from the word "papyrus"!

School was often held outdoors!

In Egypt, students used bulrushes as pens!

SYNAGOGUE

Learning at home

The school room was often attached to the synagogue.

Students dipped reeds into ink made out of soot or charcoal mixed with water, oil and gum.

School in Egypt

In the summer, school was only four hours a day.

As soon as a boy learned to read, he was given a scroll with Deuteronomy 6:4 inscribed on it: "Hear, O Israel: The Lord our God is one Lord." This was said every morning and every evening, along with a psalm, the creation story and the main part of God's law.

In Egypt, only wealthy children – both boys and girls – went to school. They learned reading, writing, math, science, religion, law and history. They usually wrote on pieces of clay pottery with reed pens and sooty ink. Egyptians used an alphabet of hieroglyphs, or symbols and pictures, to represent sounds. And, although the Jewish people lived in Egypt for some time, they were not allowed to attend Egyptian schools. Their children learned everything at home.

What was different about school back then? Jewish girls didn't go! They stayed at home and learned how to cook and care for a home and family. But some girls also learned to read and write at home. And all children learned the history and religion of their people at home.

Special Days

Just as people today worship in many different ways, so did people in Bible times. Some people, including the Egyptians, Greeks and Romans, worshiped many imaginary gods or statues called "idols." But God's people worshiped the one true God. They usually held religious holidays at planting and harvest times, to thank God for their crops.

Then God sent his people a great gift: his Son Jesus. Jesus came to be a sacrifice; he died for people's sins. People who believed Jesus was God's Son became known as Christians.

The scene on the next page shows a "bar mitzvah" at the time of Jesus. This was a special ceremony in the synagogue for thirteen-year-old Jewish boys. It showed a boy had become a "son of the Law," or an adult.

Feast of Weeks

Every year at the end of the harvest, God's people would bring gifts of food to offer as sacrifices to God. During this holiday, people remembered when Moses received God's laws at Mount Sinai.

Passover

This festival reminded God's people of a narrow escape! Once, the king of Egypt made God's people slaves. So God sent ten plagues to convince the king to let God's people go free. In the tenth plague, the oldest son in every Egyptian household died. But God passed over the houses of God's people that had lamb's blood on the doorposts. This is what God's people remembered during Passover. Christians call Jesus the "passover lamb" (1 Cor. 5:7) because he gave his life for us to save us from slavery to sin.

Feast of Tabernacles

This festival was like a big camp-out! After they escaped from Egypt, God's people wandered in the desert for 40 years! During the Feast of Tabernacles, they lived in shelters made of palm and willow branches, to remind them of the shelters they made when they were in the desert.

Sports & Music

During certain festivals, men danced all night in the temple.

Daily life in Bible times was hard work, but people did have time off and they liked to have fun just like we do today.

They played music when they celebrated special events, when they won victories in battle, when they were sad, and when mothers were having babies! Music also played a very important part in worship, as people used it to express their thanks and joy to God.

Playing games was also part of life in Bible times. Jewish people liked wrestling, and children played many games that are still played today.

The first Olympics!

The Greeks loved sports and exercise – they invented the gymnasium and the Olympic games! They also invented many of the games played in Bible lands. The Jewish people did not approve of Greek games because the Greeks dedicated their sports to pagan gods.

A chariot race was usually six miles long and the winner got a special prize.

Tops and hoops were favorite toys among children in Egypt.

Hopscotch and blind-man's bluff were popular children's games in Bible times.

Boys liked to play toss with a leather-covered ball. But they did not use sticks or bats, so there were no baseball games.

Guess what?

People had fun playing guessing games in Bible times. Samson even asked riddles at his wedding. (Answer: A kitten.)

Roughhousing

The Romans enjoyed watching gladiators and chariot racing. The Jews did not like these violent sports.

What? No prize money?

A crown of leaves was an award for winning a game.

That's much better!

David's harp music chased an evil spirit out of Saul!

Hallelujah! *Nice harmony!*

Only men from the Levite tribe sang in the temple choir.

Bigger and bigger

Oh, man, listen to this!

Awesome!

The harp started out as a small instrument. Then musicians discovered they could get a bigger sound by making the harp bigger. It got so big the harpist had to sit down to play it!

King of songs

At this rate, we'll run out of papyrus day after tomorrow!

Ooh! And how about this: "Come bless the Lord. . ."

King Solomon liked to write songs. He liked it so much, he wrote 1,005 of them!

Nice shot!

Slingshots also were popular toys, but they had to be handled carefully because they actually were weapons!

. . . it was the biggest fish!. . .

Tambourines were very popular instruments at festivals.

Traveling storytellers captured the attention of everyone with tales of God's love and exciting Bible stories.

The first trumpets, called "shophars," were made from the horns of rams. Each morning the Jewish priests blew their trumpets and the great gates of the temple were opened — a wake-up call for the whole city! (For a famous story about trumpets see Joshua 6:1-20!)

Dancing

Gee, Isaac – you're really very light on your feet!

Men and women danced separately during Bible times. Dancing was usually a part of worship.

Theatergoers

This group from Athens is terrific!

Yeah!

Greeks loved the theater and often attended plays featured by touring companies.

Travel

Getting around today is pretty easy, but that wasn't true in Bible times. Imagine living without airplanes, cars, buses and taxis!

People sometimes rode donkeys and camels, but mostly they depended on their own two feet. And they tried to travel early, before the sun got too hot. Sycamore trees were planted beside the roads to give shade to travelers. For longer trips people could rent a cart, and for the longest trips some people traveled on ships.

The main scene shows travelers in Jesus' time.

People rode camels to get across the desert.

Roads got very muddy in heavy rain showers and stopped even the best chariot drivers.

Not again! I hate this!

Luggage in Bible times had to fit on a donkey. So people put their clothes and belongings in a basket or a small leather bag.

The Romans built important roads linking major cities to Rome. These roads were usually paved with stones and dipped lower on the edges to prevent flooding.

Milestones marked how far travelers were from Rome.

People with enough money could rent carriages for traveling to another city, a bit like our taxis today!

Luxury travel

Wow! Is that the new Eagle 2000?

No! It's the new Scorpion TX, Gold Scarab edition. Nice, huh?

Soldiers rode horses or used them to pull chariots. Otherwise, a horse was a luxury in Bible times. But King Solomon had 12,000 horses! Horses and chariots were imported from Egypt.

Egyptian war chariots were the best and the most expensive in the world. They cost 7 kilograms of gold — that's about $95,000 today!